WEIRD
WEATHER &
CHANGING
CLIMATES

THIS IS A WELBECK CHILDREN'S BOOK

Text, design and illustration © Welbeck Children's Limited 2020

Published in 2020 by Welbeck Children's Limited
An imprint of the Welbeck Publishing Group
20 Mortimer Street, London W1T 3JW

A catalogue record for this book is available from the British Library.

ISBN: 978-1-78312-505-0

Printed in Dongguan, China

10 9 8 7 6 5 4 3 2 1

Executive Editor: Bryony Davies
Editor: Elly Dowsett
Design Manager: Emily Clarke
Designer: Darren Jordan
Picture Researcher: Paul Langan
Production: Nicola Davey

The publishers would like to thank the following sources for their kind permission to reproduce the pictures in this book.

ARGO /University of California: 14

Climate Central: 17

Getty Images: Mark Ralston /AFP 42; /Stacey Wescott /Chicago Tribune /TNS 33 (bottom)

Istockphoto: 5 (bottom)

Shutterstock (in order of appearance): Andrey Armyagov 4 (top), Irin-k (4 (centre), 4 Chokchai Poomichaiya (bottom), 4-5 Intrepix (background), 5 Simon Annable (top), 5 Aapsky (centre), 6-7 Andrey Armyagov, 7 Intrepix 11 Wildside (top), 11 2M media (bottom), 12-13 Irin-k, 16 Chumash Maxim (centre), 16 Sixpixx (bottom), 19 Vlada Zhi, 20 & 20-21 FloridaStock, 21 ImageBROKER, 23 ASA Studio (top left), 23 Creatsy (bottom), 23 AfriamPOE (top right), 23 Evgeny Karandaev (bottom right), 22-23 Vchal, 24-25 Chokchai Poomichaiya, 26-27 Ryan DeBeradinis, 27 AP (top), 27 Cammie Czuchnicki (bottom), 28, 28-29 Goga Shutter, 29 T Photography, 30 Corrado Baratta, 30-31 Phoutthavong Souvannachak, 31 Vladimir Wrangel, 32 Robert Cicchetti, 32-33 Daniel Maurer / EPA, 34 Ty Lim, 34-35 Marina Onokhina, 35 Ond, Chuhastock, Anatolir, Panda Vector, 36-37 Simmon Annable, 38 Valery Shanin, 38-39 Mathias Sunke, 39 Jim Barber, 40 Zvonimir Atletic (top), 40 Travelview (bottom), 40-41 Harish Tyagi /EPA, 41 ArtLovePhoto, 42 TicaC (top), 43 Johann van Trodder, 43-44 Paula French, 45 David Evison, 46 Gyvafoto, 46-47 Oticki, 47 Phant (top left), 47 Tomas Regina (centre left), 47 Gillian Pullinger (top right), Ruksutakarn Studio (centre right), 48-49 Aapsky, 50-51 Fotos593, 51 Rich Carey (top), 51 Dmytro Zinkevych (bottom), 52 Smereka, 52-53 Vchal, 53 David Dennis (top), 53 Adam Goodwillie Photos (bottom), 54 Praszkiewicz, 54-55 NadyGinzburg, 55 StreetVJ (top), 57 Photofusion (top), 57 Anticiclo (centre), 57 Jason Mintzer (bottom), 58 ppart (centre), 58 Pekka Nikonen (bottom), 60 Begun1983 (left) 60 (right) Daniele Cossu,

Peter Liddiard: 8-9, 10, 18, 26, 33 (top), 42, 56, 59, 61

NASA Climate 365 Project: 15

FSC
MIX
Paper
FSC® C144853

WEIRD WEATHER & CHANGING CLIMATES

Written by Hannah Wilson

CONTENTS

CLIMATE CRISIS

Our planet is warming up too much and too quickly, bringing wild weather and extreme temperatures. This is upsetting the delicate balance that supports life on Earth. This is called climate change and it's our fault. But because we are the cause, we can be the solution, too.

STUDYING THE SIGNS

Before we take action, let's dive deep into the oceans to find out why they are heating up and how their changing temperature damages Earth. Let's shelter from superstorms, sweat it out in scorching deserts and look up to the skies to check out the ghastly gases that are causing so many problems.

Icecaps at the poles are melting fast, sea levels are rapidly rising and heatwaves are scorching the land. The hurricanes that sweep across oceans are supercharging, and catastrophic rains are washing away farmland and towns.

GLOBAL WARMING

Earth has warmed by about 1°C since 1750 or so, when industrialisation began and factories started to burn fossil fuels. This small increase in average surface temperature is having a big effect on the health of our planet.

FOSSIL FUELS

The coal that we burn in power stations to make electricity, the petrol (oil) we burn inside cars and the gas that heats our homes are all types of fossil fuel. Coal, oil and gas formed deep underground from the fossils of plants and creatures that died millions of years ago. Fossil fuels contain carbon, and when the fuel is burnt, the carbon is released as the gas carbon dioxide (CO_2).

LAYER OF GREENHOUSE GASES

A carbon footprint measures the amount of CO_2 and other greenhouse gases that an object or activity releases. For example, a fork's carbon footprint includes the CO_2 produced by mining the metal, moulding it into shape in a factory and trucking it to the shops.

EARTH'S ATMOSPHERE

SUN

THE GREENHOUSE EFFEC

Our homes, cars and factories pump
about 40 billion tonnes of CO_2 every y
This gas then wraps around our planet and
lets the Sun's heat in, but not out, just like a
greenhouse. Methane (see pages 52–53) is also
a greenhouse gas, but its greenhouse effect
is a staggering 25 times more powerful than
CO_2. Methane is released when waste in landfill
rots and when cows burp grassy gas! These
greenhouse gases stay in the atmosphere, so
every year the 'blanket' gets thicker and thicker
and Earth gets hotter and hotter.

**SOME OF THE SUN'S HEAT
ESCAPES BACK INTO SPACE**

**SOME OF THE SUN'S HEAT BOUNCES OFF THE
GASES AND BACK TO EARTH'S SURFACE**

✠ TIP ✠

Think about the fossil fuels burnt
to light and heat your home or to
power your car. Think about the
CO_2 released by the factories
that make your clothes, toys and
food. But don't panic! You can
lower your carbon footprint –
and this book is packed with
top tips to help you.

EARTH

WEATHER AND WATER

Climate change is a global problem. Weather doesn't pay any attention to the borders of different countries. Planet Earth is one huge, connected system – and the lifeblood of that system is water.

THE WATER CYCLE

Water can be a liquid, a gas (vapour) or a solid (ice), depending on its temperature. As water is warmed by the Sun, it rises as vapour, then it cools into a liquid and falls to the ground. This happens in a constant cycle.

RAIN AND SNOW FALL FROM CLOUDS

WATER VAPOUR CONDENSES TO FORM CLOUDS

SNOW MELTS AND RUNS INTO RIVERS

WATER RUNS OFF HIGH GROUND INTO RIVERS

WATER IS WARMED BY THE SUN AND EVAPORATES FROM THE SEA

RIVERS CARRY WATER BACK TO THE OCEAN

WATER EVAPORATES FROM SOIL AND PLANTS

WATER EVAPORATES FROM RIVERS AND LAKES

WATER SEEPS THROUGH SOIL AND ROCKS AND EVENTUALLY EMPTIES INTO THE SEA

WHAT IS CLIMATE?

Climate is a regular pattern of weather over a long period of time. Different places have different climates – some are hot and dry, others are cold and wet. A freak snowstorm or a heatwave every now and then does not mean that anything drastic is happening long-term. But when weather gets weirder and weirder over a period of time, it's a sure sign that the climate is changing. And that means Earth could be in danger. In the following chapters, we'll find out why climate change is a problem and what can be done to fight it.

We need water for drinking and growing crops, but not so much of it that our homes flood. We need sunlight and heat for farming, but not so much that the land is scorched. When the climate changes, the delicate balance of life on Earth is at risk.

FACT
The number of droughts, floods and other weird weather events that happen each year around the world has doubled since 1980.

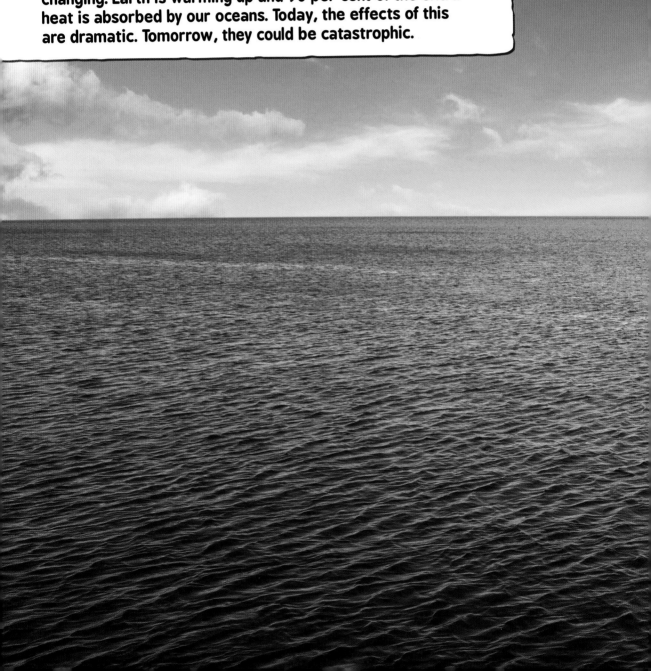

OCEAN

Almost three-quarters of our beautiful blue-green planet is covered by ocean. This huge swirling mass of water powers climates and weather systems. But the world's waters are changing. Earth is warming up and 90 per cent of the extra heat is absorbed by our oceans. Today, the effects of this are dramatic. Tomorrow, they could be catastrophic.

Most of the Sun's heat is stored in the ocean – often for hundreds of years. The ocean slowly releases some of the heat by warming the air, evaporating surface water and melting ice at the poles. But it stores more than it releases, so the ocean is constantly getting warmer.

THE RISING SEA

Over billions of years, sea levels naturally rise and fall as continents collide and ice ages come and go. But at the moment, sea levels are rising rapidly in a short space of time. Why? It's because of expanding water and melting ice, both of which are accelerated by human-made global heating.

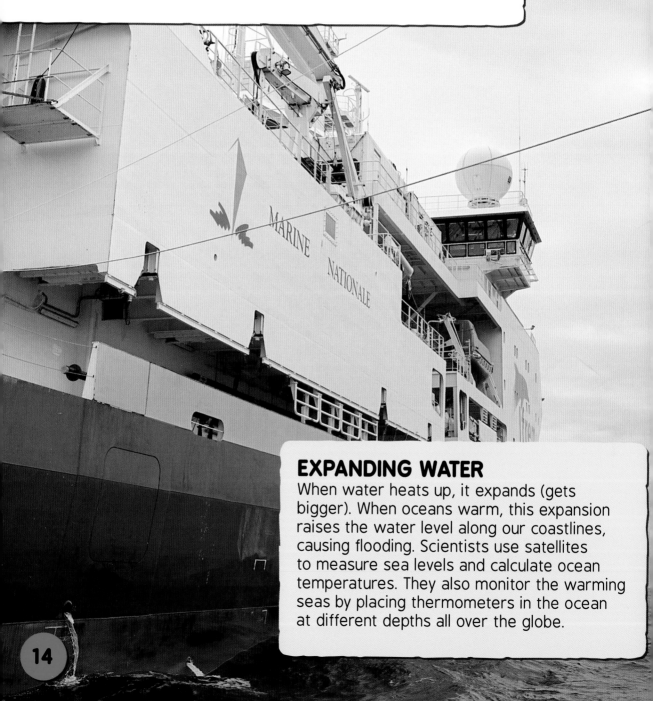

EXPANDING WATER
When water heats up, it expands (gets bigger). When oceans warm, this expansion raises the water level along our coastlines, causing flooding. Scientists use satellites to measure sea levels and calculate ocean temperatures. They also monitor the warming seas by placing thermometers in the ocean at different depths all over the globe.

MELTING ICE

The Arctic is made up of frozen seawater so when its ice melts, sea levels don't rise because no extra water enters the ocean. This is also true of the giant floating ice shelves that hug the coastline of Antarctica. However, as ice shelves collapse into the ocean, they no longer hold back the glaciers that flow across the land. These giant rivers of ice slowly melt into the sea, adding huge quantities of water to the ocean and raising sea levels. Mountain glaciers all over the world are also melting (compare the pictures below), pouring extra water into rivers, which then empty into the sea, raising levels higher.

When snow and ice melt, we lose areas of white surface cover that reflect the Sun's heat back into space. On Mount Everest in the Himalayas, as glaciers retreat, they expose the frozen bodies of mountaineers who died long ago.

COASTAL FLOODING

The sea rising by a metre or so doesn't sound too bad, right? But if you live in a low-lying country it's very bad news! Even a rise of a few centimetres would flood coastal regions all over the world. As most large cities sit by the sea, this is a big problem for millions of people.

ISLANDS AT RISK

The Maldives, a group of islands in the Indian Ocean, is the lowest-lying country in the world — only 1.8 m above sea level. Most of its 1,190 islands will be completely underwater by 2100 if sea levels continue rising at their current rate. Before that happens, though, freshwater supplies under ground will be contaminated by salty floodwater washing over the land and seeping into the rock. Maldivians are fighting climate change by creating electricity from wind turbines and solar panels, rather than relying on fossil fuels.

TIDAL TROUBLE

Tides are the daily rise and fall of sea levels, caused by the Sun and Moon's gravity. Trouble begins when a high tide occurs at the same time as a storm surge – a rising swell of water up to 8 m high caused by hurricanes. Water is pushed inland, flooding coastal regions. As sea levels rise, floods occur more frequently and devastate larger areas.

FACT

Flooding at high tide is up to 900 per cent more frequent in the USA today than it was 50 years ago.

A rise in sea levels is flooding the US state of Florida more and more frequently, swamping beachside houses. Pumps try to clear excess water, and some roads and buildings are being moved or raised. But by 2100, one out of every eight homes could be underwater.

CHANGING CURRENTS

Ocean currents are rivers of cold or warm water that continually swirl around our planet, bringing different climates and weather patterns. But the currents are slowing.

GLOBAL CONVEYOR BELT

NORTH POLE

WARM SURFACE CURRENTS

COLD DEEP-SEA CURRENTS

ATLANTIC OCEAN

PACIFIC OCEAN

EQUATOR

PACIFIC OCEAN

INDIAN OCEAN

SOUTH POLE

The global conveyor belt is the constant movement of ocean currents around the globe. At the poles, cold water sinks and travels in deep currents. When it arrives in tropical regions near the equator, it warms, rises and then delivers heat as it travels back to the poles.

ENGINE TROUBLES

The cold, deep waters at the poles are the engines that power Earth's ocean currents. As icecaps melt, more freshwater enters the polar seas. Freshwater is less dense than salty seawater so it does not sink as easily to kick-start the deep cold ocean currents. With weaker engines, the whole system of currents is slowing.

Slowing Atlantic currents bring colder winters and hotter summers to Europe. The build-up of warmer water on the east coast of the USA may deliver superstorms and destroy populations of fish such as cod.

SLOW BUT NOT STEADY

Why does it matter that ocean currents are slowing down? The ocean stores a huge amount of the Sun's heat and distributes it around the globe, ensuring that nowhere gets too hot or too cold. Without these currents spreading heat, Earth's temperatures would be more extreme, and more areas would be uninhabitable. Warm currents also bring essential rain because warm water evaporates to form clouds.

TOTALLY TRUE - OR - FOOLISHLY FALSE?

It can take 1,000 years for water to travel around the globe, completing one loop of the ocean current network.

Cold water rises and warm water sinks.

Find the answers at the back of the book

SUFFERING SEA LIFE

As the climate changes, icy habitats shrink, seas become too warm and oceans acidify. When fish populations suffer, so do the people who rely on fishing for food or to earn a living.

HARMFUL HEAT

Warming seas cause some fish to have too many male or too many female babies. This affects breeding and could wipe out entire populations. Plankton – tiny floating plants and animals – often prefer cooler water. If they die out, whole food chains could collapse because the plankton are food for fish and shrimp, which are then eaten by sharks, seals and dolphins. Polar bears are also threatened by global warming because as the Arctic sea ice shrinks, they have less space for hunting, resting and breeding.

ACID IN THE OCEAN

The sea absorbs some of the CO_2 from the air – about 30 per cent of human-produced CO_2 ends up in the ocean. This helps reduce the greenhouse effect, but it's not all good news. As the CO_2 dissolves in seawater, carbonic acid forms. Fish and squid struggle to extract oxygen from acidic water, and lobsters, crabs and oysters cannot grow strong shells. As seas acidify, corals find it hard to grow the skeletons that form reefs in tropical areas.

FACT
Coral reefs, which protect coastlines from waves, storms and floods, are home to nearly a quarter of all ocean life.

Tiny algae live on corals, giving them energy and often colour. Unusually warm seas are killing the algae, which starves the corals and turns them white. This 'coral bleaching' has killed half of Australia's Great Barrier Reef since 2016.

FIGHT CLIMATE CHANGE!

The battle to protect our planet is all about reducing CO_2 by burning fewer fossil fuels. You can lower your carbon footprint with a few simple steps.

✵ TIP ✵

Avoid polyester or nylon clothes – each time they're washed, up to 700,000 tiny microfibres of plastic go down the drain and can end up in rivers and seas.

WHAT YOU CAN DO

✓ Reduce, reuse and recycle your stuff. This means fewer fossil fuels are burnt to power the factories that make clothes, toys, food packaging and all sorts of other things.

✓ Switch off. Save energy to save the planet.

✓ Take your own water bottle and shopping bag.

✓ Reduce the amount of new things you buy.

✓ Check out charity shops for second-hand treasures.

✓ Reuse as much as possible, then donate your stuff so others can reuse it.

✓ Recycle – don't dump in polluting landfill.

REDUCE · REUSE · RECYCLE

AWESOME ACTIVITIES

Save money – and the planet – by making your own gifts, wrapping paper and cards. Then get busy with some simple ocean experiments.

GREETING CARDS

Stick pictures from old magazines onto scraps of card.

BEACH CLEAN-UP

Collect some rubbish from the beach to stop it trashing the ocean.

ACID OCEAN

Find two similar seashells. Put one in a glass of water and one in a glass of white vinegar (which is acidic). Compare them after 24 hours.

ICEBERG MELT

Fill a glass with water and ice cubes (icebergs). Mark the glass to show the level of the water. Does it rise when the ice has melted?

ARE YOU SEA SMART?

Find the answers at the back of the book

Test your knowledge...

1. What increases when sea levels rise?

- **A.** Number of fish
- **B.** Coastal flooding
- **C.** Tropical storms

2. What happens to ocean currents as Earth gets warmer?

- **A.** They slow down
- **B.** They speed up
- **C.** They disappear

3. What is formed when CO_2 dissolves in the ocean?

- **A.** Arctic acid
- **B.** Atlantic acid
- **C.** Carbonic acid

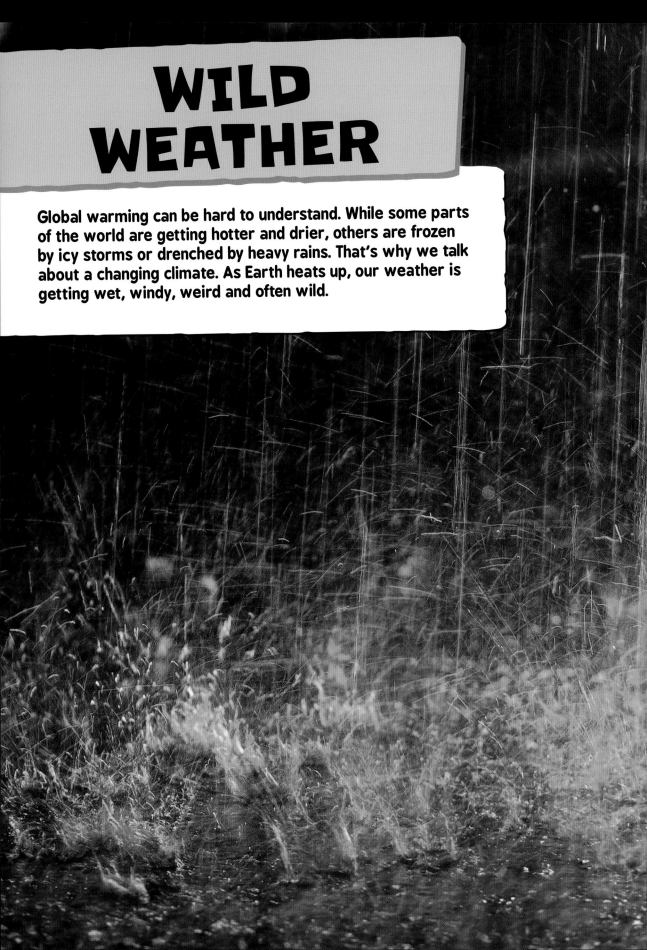

WILD WEATHER

Global warming can be hard to understand. While some parts of the world are getting hotter and drier, others are frozen by icy storms or drenched by heavy rains. That's why we talk about a changing climate. As Earth heats up, our weather is getting wet, windy, weird and often wild.

Since the 1950s, Earth has experienced heavier rainfall and more frequent storms. Sewers and drains overflow, unable to cope with sudden, intense downpours. Rivers struggle to hold the extra water, bursting their banks to flood the surrounding land.

WILD WINDS

When hot, moist air rises from tropical oceans, it can gather into swirling storm systems. These hurricanes, also known as cyclones or typhoons, deliver devastating rain, wind and waves.

HUGE HURRICANES

Many large rainclouds swirled together over warm oceans gather more energy from winds powered by the Earth's rotation. These hurricanes, perhaps 500 km wide, storm across the ocean, gaining even more energy from the water.

COOL AIR DESCENDS

RINGS OF THICK, SWIRLING CLOUDS

WARM AIR SPIRALS UP AROUND THE EYE

EYE – A CALM CENTRAL AREA 30–65 KM WIDE

FACT
In 2017, Hurricane Maria doubled in strength to a deadly category 5 hurricane in less than 24 hours. The island of Dominica in the Caribbean Sea was devastated.

When cyclone Nargis struck Myanmar, Southeast Asia, in 2008, it sent a surge of floodwater 40 km inland. More than 84,000 people died and 53,000 went missing. Some towns and villages were wiped out.

TWISTING TORNADOES

A tornado is a rotating funnel of air that spins to the ground from a storm cloud. Every year from March to June, these storms rampage through the USA's 'Tornado Alley'. Warming seas in the nearby Gulf of Mexico are creating more and more storm clouds. Scientists are unsure if this will bring more tornadoes – it depends how winds are affected. But the warming could shift Tornado Alley eastwards, towards more densely populated regions.

FACT
At least 1,200 tornadoes hit the USA each year. Spinning at up to 480 km/h, they tear through homes, whisk away cars and can even suck water from rivers!

EXTREME RAINFALL

As the ocean warms, more and more moisture rises from its surface. Our skies store the water, whisk it along in the wind and then dump it on towns and fields – sometimes with devastating consequences.

DESTRUCTIVE DOWNPOUR

In cities, rain can't sink into roads and buildings so it washes into drains, which often overflow with harmful waste water. In the countryside, heavy rains destroy farmers' crops, causing food shortages. Water-soaked hillsides can slip, sending landslides several kilometres wide crashing downhill. Deforestation increases landslides because the soil is no longer knitted together with tree roots.

FACT

Rainfall in the Amazon Rainforest has increased over the last few decades as a direct result of the warming of the Atlantic Ocean.

SUDDEN SOAKING

Most rain is made from water that has evaporated from the sea. But evaporation also happens on land, as moisture rises from soil, plants, rivers and lakes. As Earth warms, this can happen very quickly, leaving areas sucked dry of all moisture. Weirdly, in parts of India, some of these droughts end with intense rain. The parched land has been baked so hard that it cannot easily absorb the water, and so it floods. Climate change will bring more of these unpredictable weather events.

A monsoon is a season of heavy rain that happens in many tropical countries. Increasing amounts of moisture from the warming Indian Ocean are fuelling monsoons in India. Water is needed for growing food, but too much can wipe out crops.

TOTALLY TRUE
- OR -
FOOLISHLY FALSE?

☐ Experts are 90 per cent certain that climate change will bring heavier and more frequent rainfall.

☐ A monsoon season is a period of severe drought.

Find the answers at the back of the book

RIVER FLOODING

Rivers tumble down hills and rush down mountains, then meander over lower and lower ground until they empty into the sea. As rains increase and the hills are soaked like sponges, rivers flow more furiously, causing more flooding.

BURSTING BANKS

With heavier rainfall running off high ground and rising sea levels pushing up from the coast, rivers are struggling to contain the extra water. Clearing vegetation for building or farming doesn't help, as soil — no longer held together by roots — washes into rivers, leaving even less space for the water. When the rivers finally burst their banks, muddy floodwaters devastate nearby towns, cities and fields.

FACT

Flash floods happen very quickly, sending walls of water up to 6 m high rushing across the land.

LIVES AT RISK

Poorer countries around the equator will suffer most from climate change. These tropical regions will face higher temperatures, more powerful hurricanes, heavier rain and flooding. When rivers burst their banks and swamp homes and farmland, people in poorer countries do not have the money to start new lives elsewhere. They struggle to find food and rebuild homes, and the lack of clean water causes diseases such as cholera.

Four hundred million people in 11 countries along the River Nile in Africa depend on the river. As rainfall increases in the Ethiopian Highlands (the river's main source), many homes and farms are being devastated by more extreme flooding.

DEEP FREEZE

So, if our planet is warming, why are some parts of the world being buried in snowstorms or frozen by icy blizzards? Climate change causes more extreme weather – and that can mean extreme cold, too.

POLAR VORTEX

The icy winds that swirl around the poles are known as polar vortices. In January 2019, the Arctic polar vortex swept much farther south than usual, freezing parts of eastern North America and dumping snow in the normally warm southern states of the USA. The vortex was affected partly by a change in winds caused by warming seas, but mostly by a disruption in the jet stream.

JET-STREAM JITTERS

The jet stream is a fast-flowing 'river' of wind that occurs where cold polar air meets warmer tropical air. As the poles warm due to global warming, the temperature difference at this boundary decreases, causing the jet stream to slow or move in sharp bends. One of these bends pulled the Arctic vortex southwards, bringing the deep freeze to North America in 2019. As jet streams slow, vortices and other weather systems will hang around for longer than usual.

STABLE POLAR VORTEX

COLD AIR IS CONTAINED

STRONG JET STREAM

WAVY POLAR VORTEX

COLD AIR MOVES SOUTH

WEAK JET STREAM

WARM AIR MOVES NORTH

In January 2019, the polar vortex brought temperatures of −46°C to the city of Chicago in the USA. Train tracks had to be set on fire to stop them freezing!

FIGHT CLIMATE CHANGE!

Think green to stop weather becoming extreme! Here are suggestions for how you can make a difference and look after planet Earth.

WHAT YOU CAN DO

Think about how things are made. Plastic uses oil, drilled from below ground and processed in factories. Use less plastic in order to produce less CO_2.

- ✓ Cut back on single-use plastic (plastic that is used once before being thrown or recycled).

- ✓ Travel by bus, train or bike – rather than by car – to reduce your carbon footprint.

- ✓ Organise a school cake sale to raise money for countries affected by flooding or hurricanes.

- ✓ Choose unpackaged fruit and veg at the shops.

- ✓ Take charge of your classroom's recycling.

- ✓ Use your own lunch box for takeaway food.

FACT
It can take 1,000 years for some types of plastic to break down in landfill!

AWESOME ACTIVITIES

Turn your eyes to the skies to watch for wild weather.
Then make some storms of your own!

! Ask an adult to help you with any cutting.

RAINCATCHER

Collect rain in the bottom half of a plastic bottle. Every day, dip in a ruler to measure and record any rainfall, then empty the bottle.

STORM IN A GLASS

Squirt shaving foam onto water in a glass.

HOMEMADE HURRICANE

Pour some water into a bowl, stir it quickly round and round and add drops of food dye. What happens to the colour?

Add spoonfuls of water coloured with food dye onto your foam 'cloud'. How much water can it hold before it 'rains'?

ARE YOU A WEATHER WHIZZ KID?

Test your knowledge...   Find the answers at the back of the book

1. Where is 'Tornado Alley'?

- **A.** Mexico
- **B.** Myanmar
- **C.** USA

2. What increases the risk of river flooding and landslides?

- **A.** Deforestation
- **B.** Planting trees
- **C.** Cholera

3. What does the weather become because of climate change?

- **A.** More extreme
- **B.** More predictable
- **C.** Calmer

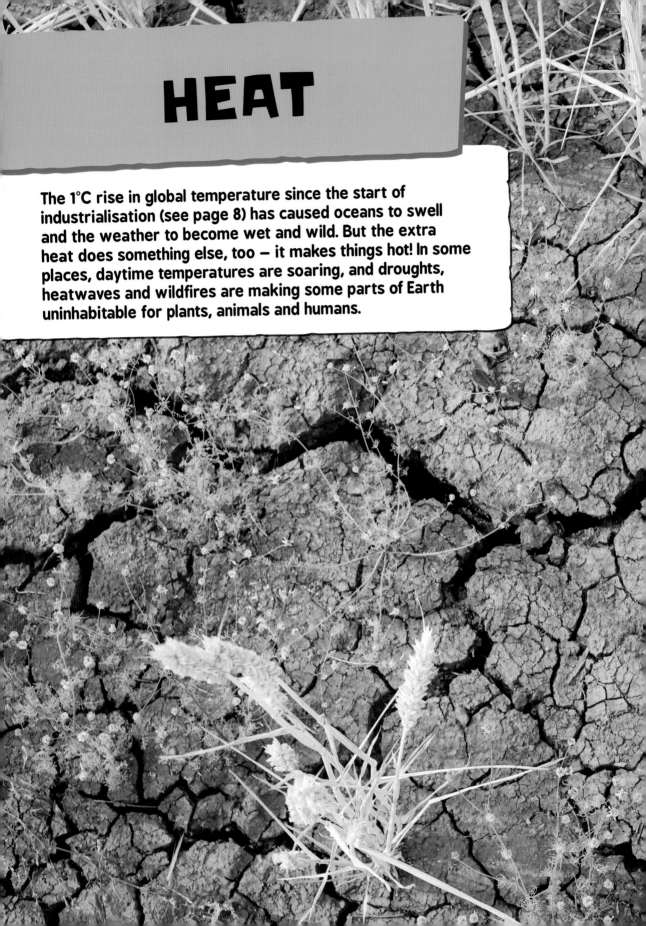

HEAT

The 1°C rise in global temperature since the start of industrialisation (see page 8) has caused oceans to swell and the weather to become wet and wild. But the extra heat does something else, too – it makes things hot! In some places, daytime temperatures are soaring, and droughts, heatwaves and wildfires are making some parts of Earth uninhabitable for plants, animals and humans.

As Earth heats up, droughts become more extreme, and farmers struggle to find water for crops and cattle. This causes food shortages and, in the worst cases, famine – a widespread lack of food that can cause the death of thousands of people.

DROUGHT

Overall, climate change brings an increase in rainfall. But in some parts of the world it brings less rain. These places are drying up, and people are struggling to find enough water to drink and to grow crops or raise animals.

DRIER AND DRIER

Droughts are a normal part of dry seasons in many parts of the world. But climate change is making some droughts more extreme. As ocean and air currents change and slow down, there is less rainfall in some areas and dry seasons hang around for longer. Warmer temperatures mean that more moisture evaporates from the land, drying out vegetation and soil. The sudden, heavy downpours caused by climate change run off the surface of the hard, baked land. This run-off may fill rivers and lakes, but it doesn't soak into the soil where it is needed for thirsty crops.

FACT

The Sahara is the world's biggest warm-weather desert. It has expanded by 10 per cent since 1920, partly due to climate change.

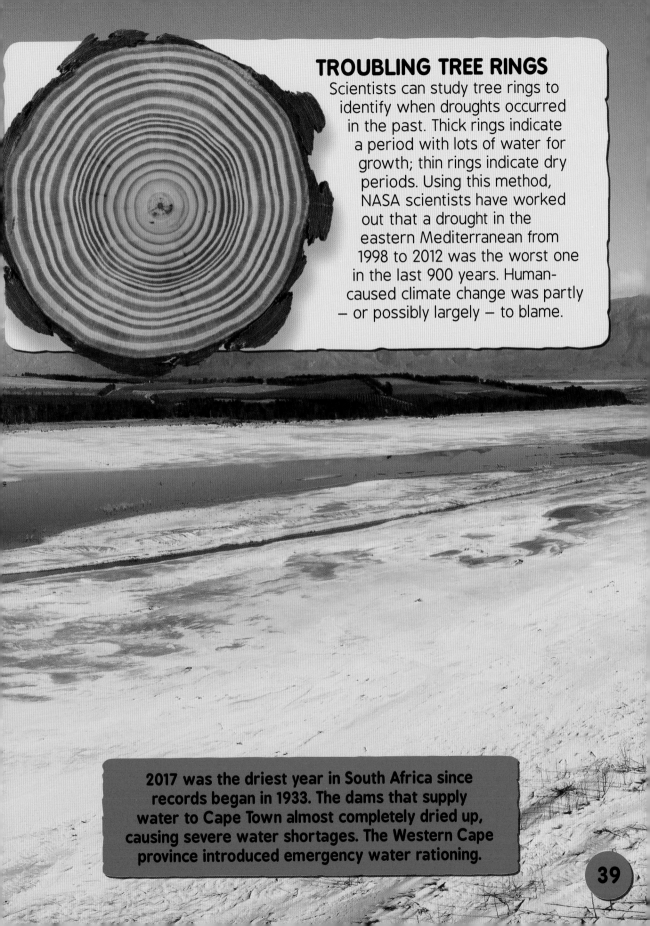

TROUBLING TREE RINGS

Scientists can study tree rings to identify when droughts occurred in the past. Thick rings indicate a period with lots of water for growth; thin rings indicate dry periods. Using this method, NASA scientists have worked out that a drought in the eastern Mediterranean from 1998 to 2012 was the worst one in the last 900 years. Human-caused climate change was partly – or possibly largely – to blame.

2017 was the driest year in South Africa since records began in 1933. The dams that supply water to Cape Town almost completely dried up, causing severe water shortages. The Western Cape province introduced emergency water rationing.

HEATWAVES

If temperatures continue to rise at their current rate, some parts of Earth will be too hot for humans to live in by the end of this century. Extreme heatwaves harm humans, destroy crops and spread disease.

TOO HOT TO HANDLE

Humans keep cool by sweating – releasing moisture from our skin into the air. But we cannot sweat easily if the air is already very humid (full of moisture). So when a heatwave strikes humid regions, people get dangerously hot. About 1.5 billion people live in the south Asian countries of Pakistan, India and Bangladesh – many in poverty. It's been predicted that by 2100, the heat and humidity in some parts of this region will be so high that if people go outside unprotected, they will die within a few hours.

Many people around the world have to work outside for long periods in fields or on building sites. They will be extremely vulnerable to the effects of heatwaves.

DEADLY DISEASE

Tropical diseases begin in the tropics – the hot region around the equator. But as human activity warms Earth, the tropics are spreading further north and further south of the equator – and so are the diseases. Malaria is carried by a tropical mosquito. As the insect's habitat expands, the disease will spread to more areas of the world.

FACT

When an extreme heatwave hit India in 2015, about 2,500 people died. The capital, New Delhi, neared 45°C, causing some roads to melt.

TOTALLY TRUE - OR - FOOLISHLY FALSE?

Green energy uses renewable resources that don't run out, such as wind, sunlight and ocean waves.

Green energy uses energy produced in power stations from coal, oil or gas.

Find the answers at the back of the book

WILDFIRES

Wildfires are nature's way of clearing vegetation for new growth, but climate change is bringing more than nature can cope with. And when fires break out, they spread faster and further, fuelled by drier conditions.

CHANGING WEATHER PATTERNS

In the Pacific Ocean, water on the surface is warmed by the Sun and then pushed east by wind. How strong or weak these winds are makes a big difference to the water temperature, and to the resulting weather.

WARM WATER EVAPORATES IN THE EAST

NORMAL CONDITIONS

WINDS PUSH WARM WATER EASTWARDS

'EL NINO' – WARMER OCEAN CURRENTS

WARM WATER EVAPORATES IN THE MIDDLE

WEAK WINDS PUSH WARM WATER LESS FAR EAST

WARM WATER EVAPORATES FURTHER EAST

'LA NINA' – COOLER OCEAN CURRENTS

STRONG WINDS PUSH WARM WATER EVEN FURTHER EASTWARDS

CALIFORNIA BURNING

In 2018, a series of 8,527 wildfires ravaged the western USA state of California for several months. More than 80 people died and almost 14,000 homes were destroyed. It costs millions to put out the fires and rebuild. Wildfires also release carbon dioxide (CO_2), increasing the greenhouse effect that leads to further climate change. The smoke contains toxic carbon monoxide and other gases that harm humans and pollute our environment. What's more, fire-scorched landscapes are more vulnerable to landslides and flooding.

FACT
California's 2018 wildfires released 68 million tonnes of CO_2 — almost the same amount of CO_2 generated from electricity production in the state in a year.

Weaker winds and warmer currents are a phenomenon called 'El Nino'. Stronger winds and cooler currents are called 'La Nina'. These occur naturally but climate change is intensifying them. In 2018, a supercharged La Nina made California hotter and drier, which had a direct impact on deadly wildfires.

WILDLIFE AT RISK

Creatures all over the world are affected by climate change as their habitats shrink or move. It's not just polar bears in the Arctic that suffer as our planet warms. Animals in hot climates are struggling with empty waterholes, scorched plants and dangerously high temperatures.

HUNGRY AND THIRSTY

As severe droughts become more common, many waterholes in southern Africa are drying up. This is a huge problem for elephants, which need to drink between 150 and 300 litres of water every day. The lack of water and excess heat affects plant life, too. In Australia, shrubs and grasses are changing or disappearing altogether. Because of this, many rock wallabies are no longer getting a proper diet, and their population is reducing.

FACT
If Earth continues to heat up at its current rate, 80 per cent of mammals and 86 per cent of birds in a 2.4 million km^2 area of southern Africa will be at risk of extinction by the 2080s.

ON THE MOVE

Shrubs in North America are creeping closer to the warming Arctic, followed by the moose and snowshoe hares that eat them. On mountainsides, plants and animals are climbing higher as snowlines retreat. Mackerel in the Atlantic have swum northwards to cooler waters near Iceland. Not all wildlife adapts easily, and towns often block the path of animals forced to move home. As spring arrives earlier, flowers are blooming too soon for the bees that feed from and pollinate them.

Turtles bury their eggs in sand and the temperature determines whether hatchlings are male or female. In many of their habitats, warmer sand is causing an imbalance of females.

African wild dogs rely on cool mornings and evenings for hunting. As temperatures rise, their pups go hungry. From 1989 to 2000, about five pups in each den survived for at least a year. By 2012, when it was 1.1°C warmer, only three survived.

FIGHT CLIMATE CHANGE!

Think about the food and water you consume, and go green to battle Earth's warming. Vegetables are better for the planet than meat, and water is precious, so go easy on the tap!

WHAT YOU CAN DO

Saving water also saves energy, because electricity is used to clean and pump your water.

✓ Turn off the tap when brushing teeth and take showers, not baths.

✓ Avoid electric fans and air-conditioners. Keep cool by closing curtains and blinds.

✓ Reduce your carbon footprint by eating less meat.

✓ Collect rainwater for watering plants.

✓ Use a green-energy supplier to power your home.

FACT
Our 'water footprint' is how much water we use for washing and making all the things we consume. In the UK, the average person's daily footprint is more than 4,500 litres – about 50 bathtubs!

AWESOME ACTIVITIES

Go veggie for a day and follow these steps to keep wildlife happy in the heat!

MEAT-FREE MEAL
Make a vegetarian pizza.

BIRD BATH
Fill a shallow tub or tray with stones and water for birds.

FACT
A vegetarian diet produces about 3.8 kg of greenhouse gases every day. A meat-rich diet produces 7.2 kg – partly because cows burp methane! (See page 52.)

BEE GARDEN
Plant an outdoor pot with bee-friendly flowers.

HOT OR COLD?
Put a thermometer outside in the shade. Record the temperature at the same time each day for a week during different seasons.

ARE YOU A HEAT HOTSHOT?

Test your knowledge...

Find the answers at the back of the book

1. What does run-off do?

- **A.** Soak into soil
- **B.** Flow over ground
- **C.** Form whirlpools

2. Which region is expanding?

- **A.** The Arctic
- **B.** The tropics
- **C.** Australia

3. What is happening to wildfires?

- **A.** They are becoming more frequent
- **B.** They are getting smaller
- **C.** They are spreading more slowly

AIR

Swirling all around us and moving in and out of our lungs, air is a vital life-force – for us and for our planet. But factories, power stations and cars are pumping harmful gases into the air we breathe. Some are toxic. They damage our health and can devastate plants, animals and wild spaces. Other gases are non-toxic to our bodies, but by wrapping around Earth, they cause devastating climate change.

Vehicles and power stations belch out the non-toxic greenhouse gas carbon dioxide (CO_2), as well as toxic carbon monoxide, sulphur dioxide and nitrogen oxides.

TREE POWER

Trees help our environment because their roots hold soil together, preventing floods and landslides. But trees protect us in another, even more important way. They pump oxygen into the air and suck up harmful carbon dioxide (CO_2).

FACT

Every year, Earth's forests suck up more than 2 billion tonnes of carbon. One quarter of that is absorbed by the Amazon Rainforest, which covers 6 million km^2 and produces more than 20 per cent of Earth's oxygen.

OUR ATMOSPHERE

The air that wraps around Earth is mostly nitrogen gas. About one-fifth is oxygen — the gas that plants and animals need for life. Almost 1 per cent is argon, and other gases make up even tinier slices. Carbon dioxide, that troublesome greenhouse gas, is less than one tenth of 1 per cent of our air.

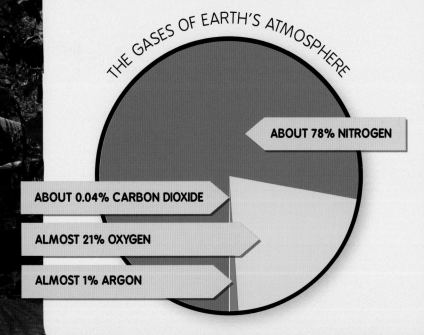

THE GASES OF EARTH'S ATMOSPHERE

ABOUT 78% NITROGEN

ABOUT 0.04% CARBON DIOXIDE

ALMOST 21% OXYGEN

ALMOST 1% ARGON

PLANTS THAT PROTECT

When we breathe, we absorb oxygen and expel CO_2. At night, plants and trees also take in oxygen and give off CO_2, but they reverse this process during the day. As they photosynthesise, they use sunlight to absorb CO_2 and produce oxygen. Overall, they absorb much more CO_2 than they produce, and they release 10 times more oxygen than they use. So this makes plants and trees great planet protectors.

Deforestation is bad news for our planet. When trees are chopped down, they can no longer absorb harmful CO_2. In fact, when they rot or are burnt as fuel, they release it. In the Amazon Rainforest, an area three times the size of the UK has been deforested since 1970, mainly for cattle grazing.

FACT
If an object or activity is 'carbon neutral', it means that no CO_2 is released when making or doing it. To achieve this, some people 'off-set' their carbon footprint by planting CO_2-sucking trees.

METHANE

Like carbon dioxide (CO_2), methane is a greenhouse gas that traps heat on Earth. But landfills and farms are pumping it out at an alarming level. And there's an even greater climate calamity lurking in the frozen permafrost at our poles.

WHAT IS METHANE?

Methane is a non-toxic flammable gas, 25 times more powerful than CO_2. It is released by rotting organic matter (material from plants, bacteria or tiny creatures) when there is no oxygen present. So methane leaks from rubbish buried deep in landfills and from the rotting grass inside cows' stomachs, which is released in farts or burps! The 'natural gas' used to heat our homes is also up to 90 per cent methane.

FACT
Worldwide, farm animals produce about 15 per cent of all human-caused greenhouse gases.

THAWING PERMAFROST

At the poles and high in the mountains, the ground is permanently frozen. The soil of this 'permafrost' contains organic matter. As icy regions warm, the permafrost is thawing and the organic material within is being released and it rots. This process releases thousands of tonnes of methane (and CO_2) into the air, accelerating climate change.

FACT
One study predicts that by 2100, the thawing permafrost could have released 37 billion tonnes of CO_2 and 1 billion tonnes of methane.

It's easy to see the methane that bubbles up through lakes, but it's not easy to collect and measure it. Scientists visit lakes in Canada, where bubbles of methane are trapped in the ice like frozen jellyfish. After chipping away at the ice, the gas can be funnelled into bottles.

CITY SMOG

Do you ever breathe in smelly, hazy air that gives you a sore throat or cough? That's air pollution. In cities, cars and factories pump out toxic gases such as carbon monoxide. Inside many homes, black smoke billows from cooking fires. Air pollution causes all sort of illnesses.

THE PARTICULATE PROBLEM

Car exhaust pipes and factories also release tiny bits of soot called particulates. These are too small to see, but the tiniest ones are the most harmful. PM 2.5s are particulates that are smaller than 2.5 micrometres — about 30 times narrower than a hair on your head. Unlike larger particulates, PM 2.5s are not stopped by nose hairs or expelled with a cough. They can pass through the walls of the lungs and into the bloodstream, where they travel around the body and cause health problems.

Dutch inventor Daan Roosegaarde's 7-m-tall air purifier sucks in city smog and pumps out clean air. This 'smog vacuum cleaner' also collects the dirty particulates and compresses them into gemstones that are used to make jewellery. Filtered smog is about 40 per cent carbon — the same stuff that diamonds are made of!

CLEAN AND GREEN

Petrol-powered vehicles emit polluting smoke and soot because their engines burn petrol (a fossil fuel). Electric cars and buses powered by hydrogen fuel cells do not use combustion (burning) for power. These 'zero emission' vehicles do not pollute our cities, but they do use energy to create the electricity or hydrogen that powers them. To combat climate change, this energy should come from a green, clean, renewable source.

FACT

All 16,000 buses and all 22,000 taxis in Shenzhen, China, are electric. Making the taxis electric reduced carbon emissions by 440,000 tonnes a year!

TOTALLY TRUE - OR - FOOLISHLY FALSE?

Electric cars and buses are much noisier than petrol-powered vehicles.

Certain trees, such as elms and ashes, can filter out air pollutants, reducing city smog.

Find the answers at the back of the book

ACID RAIN

Remember the cycle that transports water around the world through oceans, rivers and the air? (See page 10.) Because it's all connected, when the air is polluted it means that water becomes polluted, too.

TOXIC RAIN, SNOW AND DUST

Lightning produces nitrogen oxides and volcanoes belch sulphur dioxide, but most of these gases come from people burning fossil fuels. When they mix with oxygen and water in the sky, they form acids that fall to the ground in rain, snow and hail.

WINDS BLOW THE ACID PARTICLES LONG DISTANCES

THE ACID FALLS WITH RAIN, SNOW OR EVEN DUST

THE GASES MIX WITH WATER AND OXYGEN TO FORM ACIDS

POWER STATIONS AND VEHICLES EMIT NITROGEN OXIDE AND SULPHUR DIOXIDE GASES

RIVERS, LAKES AND SOIL ACIDIFY, HARMING FISH, INSECTS, PLANTS AND TREES

HABITATS IN DANGER

Acid is corrosive – it wears materials away. Pummelled by too much acid rain, marble statues appear to melt and iron railings rust. But our wild spaces suffer the most. As soils acidify, nutrients are worn away, and plants and trees struggle to grow and even die. The acidic rainwater that runs off the land into lakes and rivers kills fish and their eggs. Delicate insects also die as their habitats acidify, affecting animals further up the food chain.

Graveyards of trees carpet the landscapes of areas affected by acid rain.

FACT

In the 1980s, sulphur emissions from power stations in the UK blew across the North Sea and fell in acid rain in Norway, wiping out salmon and trout populations. Today, Norway pours 45,000 tonnes of lime into its rivers and lakes every year to make them less acidic.

FIGHT CLIMATE CHANGE!

We can't control the wind, but we can control what we pump into it. So take a deep breath – we're going green to keep our air clean.

WHAT YOU CAN DO

Reducing energy reduces the pollution created to make it. Think about indoor air, too. What pollutes your home?

✓ Try eco liquids for cleaning, not harmful chemical sprays.

✓ Walk or cycle to school to avoid pollution-heavy cars.

✓ Cut down on heating – put on another jumper instead!

✓ Use an extractor fan and open a window when cooking.

✗ Say no to wood-burning stoves and open fires.

AWESOME ACTIVITIES

Investigate the air quality in your home, then plant some natural air purifiers. They make great presents, too!

POLLUTION PLATE
Smear petroleum jelly over a white piece of plastic. After three days, use a magnifying glass to examine any particulates stuck to it.

PLANT PURIFIER
Bring ivy, spider plants and peace lilies inside to filter your indoor air.

TREE TIME
Plant a tree to suck up CO_2.

AIR CHECKER
Visit aqicn.org to check the
Air Quality Index for your
home town.

0-50
GOOD
= Air quality index
= Air pollution level

MODERATE

51-100

151-200
UNHEALTHY

101-150

**UNHEALTHY FOR
SENSITIVE GROUPS**

300+
HAZARDOUS

201-300
**VERY
UNHEALTHY**

FACT
The Air Quality
Index (AQI) uses
measurements of
particulates and polluting
gases to give a colour-coded
number for cities around
the world. Green means
clean air, yellow means
moderate and red is
unhealthy.

ARE YOU AIR AWARE?
Test your knowledge...

Find the answers at the back of the book

1. What is the most
common gas in
our atmosphere?

   A. Nitrogen

   B. Oxygen

   C. Carbon
   dioxide

2. What produces methane?

   A. Rotting organic
   matter with oxygen

   B. Rotting organic
   matter with no
   oxygen

   C. Cowpats

3. Why are very small
particulates of pollution
harmful?

   A. They can pass through
   the walls of our lungs

   B. They are invisible

   C. They smell bad

59

A GREEN FUTURE

Your future is in the hands of politicians and business leaders around the world. They can prevent a climate catastrophe by cutting carbon emissions. But they need to act seriously — and right now! You can help persuade them.

�ख TIP ✖

You can't be 100 per cent green all the time. But do your best as often as possible — and enjoy helping the planet when you can. Good luck!

THE OZONE BATTLE

In the 1980s, scientists realised that certain chemicals in aerosol sprays were eroding the ozone layer. This layer of ozone gas shields us from the Sun's ultraviolet rays, which can cause skin cancer. Governments banned the chemicals, and slowly the holes in the ozone layer began to close up. Proof that if governments work together quickly, they can protect our planet!

FACT

In August 2018, Swedish 15-year-old Greta Thunberg was worried about a heatwave and forest fires in northern Europe. Day after day, she sat outside government buildings in Stockholm to protest against climate change and she sparked a worldwide movement.

Today, Greta travels (by train or boat) to different countries, telling politicians: 'I want you to panic... And then I want you to act.'

CRAZY COOLING?

There have been many outlandish ideas for cooling Earth by reflecting heat away from it – for example, painting the roof of every building white or growing crops with shiny leaves. But this meddling could do more harm than good. Here are some more crazy ideas.

GIANT SPACE MIRRORS SO MORE HEAT IS REFLECTED INTO SPACE

CLOUD THINNING SO CIRRUS CLOUDS TRAP LESS HEAT

AEROSOL INJECTION OF REFLECTIVE PARTICLES INTO THE STRATOSPHERE SO HEAT BOUNCES OFF

MARINE CLOUD BRIGHTENING: SHIPS SPRAY SALT SO CLOUDS REFLECT MORE HEAT

OCEAN MIRROR EFFECT: SHIPS RELEASE TINY BUBBLES SO THE SEA REFLECTS MORE HEAT

The best way to stop global warming is to address the cause and reduce greenhouse gas emissions. In 2015, many countries committed to the Paris Agreement. It aims to prevent global temperatures from rising more than 2°C above pre-industrialisation levels this century. This will require governments to make dramatic changes right now.

GLOSSARY

ACID
A chemical substance, often found dissolved in water, that can break down other materials or react with them. Lemon juice and vinegar are acidic. Sulphuric acid is a powerful acid that can cause burns.

ATMOSPHERE
A layer of gases around a planet, moon or star that is held in place by the force of gravity.

CARBON DIOXIDE (CO2)
A colourless, odourless gas released when fossil fuels such as coal, oil and gas are burnt. Volcanoes produce CO_2, and animals and humans breathe it out.

CARBON FOOTPRINT
The amount of carbon dioxide and other greenhouse gases that an object or activity produces during its whole 'lifetime'.

CLIMATE
The average pattern of weather in a place over a long period of time.

CONTAMINATED
Spoiled or made dirty by the addition of a harmful or unwanted substance.

CONTINENTS
Huge sections of land that move about on top of Earth's hot liquid interior. There are seven continents, most containing a collection of different countries: Africa, Antarctica, Asia, Oceania, Europe, North America and South America.

DEFORESTATION
The cutting down of many trees, reducing the size of a natural forest.

DROUGHT
A long period of time with no or very little rainfall.

ECOSYSTEM
The plants and animals of a certain area that live together and affect each other. A small garden pond or a huge forest each have their own complex ecosystem.

EMISSION
A substance, often a gas, that is released into the atmosphere, often from a factory or vehicle.

EVAPORATE
To change, when heated, from a liquid to a gas.

FOSSIL FUEL
Natural oil, gas or coal, which formed underground millions of years ago from decomposing plants and animals. Fossil fuels contain a large amount of carbon.

GILLS
Slit-like openings on a fish's body. Water passes out through the gills once oxygen has been taken from it.

GLACIER
A large mass of ice that moves slowly downhill over land, often through mountain valleys.

GREEN
Environmentally friendly and aiming to protect, not harm, planet Earth.

GREEN ENERGY
Energy created from renewable resources (such as wind, wave and solar power) rather than from non-renewable, polluting fossil fuels.

GREENHOUSE GAS
A gas such as carbon dioxide or methane that wraps around our planet, keeping it warm. The gases create the same effect as a greenhouse – they let heat in but not out.

HEATWAVE
A period of unusually hot weather.

ICE AGE
A period lasting thousands of years in which varying amounts of Earth's surface are covered with ice. As there is ice at Earth's poles today, we are currently experiencing an ice age.

INDUSTRIALISATION
When countries or large groups of people move from a rural farming life to mining and gathering materials and making products inside factories.

LANDFILL
An area or pit where non-recyclable waste is dumped and stored.

METHANE
A powerful greenhouse gas produced when plant matter decomposes with no oxygen present. Natural gas is mostly methane.

OXYGEN
A colourless, odourless gas, mainly produced by plants. Animals and plants need oxygen to live.

PARTICULATE
A tiny bit of a material, often released into the air when the material is burnt.

POLES
The North Pole, in the Arctic, is Earth's most northerly point. The South Pole, in Antarctica, is Earth's most southerly point.

POLLINATE
To transfer pollen (a powder-like substance) from a plant's male part to another plant's female part. This fertilises plants, enabling them to create seeds to grow new plants.

REPRODUCTION
When creatures create babies, usually by the joining of a male and a female.

SEA LEVEL
The average global surface height of the ocean. Satellites can determine the average distance the surface lies above Earth's centre. Tide gauges measure local sea levels in different regions around the world.

SOLAR PANEL
A panel with special materials that absorb energy from sunlight and turn it into electricity.

THAW
To melt when warmed, changing from hard frozen matter into a liquid or soft material.

TOXIC
Poisonous and likely to cause harm to plants or animals.

TROPICAL
Of or relating to the hot wet regions surrounding the equator, which is the imaginary line circling Earth's middle.

VAPOUR
Tiny drops of liquid, often water, that hang in the air. Mist is water vapour.

WIND TURBINE
A rotating device with blades that are spun by the wind to create energy that can be turned into electricity.

ANSWERS

PAGE 19
OCEAN: TOTALLY TRUE OR FOOLISHLY FALSE?

True: It can take 1,000 years for water to travel around the globe, completing one loop of the ocean current network.

The second statement is false.

PAGE 23
ARE YOU SEA SMART?
1B, 2A, 3C

PAGE 29
WILD WEATHER: TOTALLY TRUE OR FOOLISHLY FALSE?

True: Experts are 90% certain that climate change will bring heavier and more frequent rainfall.

The second statement is false.

PAGE 35
ARE YOU A WEATHER WHIZZ KID?
1C, 2A, 3A

PAGE 41
HEAT: TOTALLY TRUE OR FOOLISHLY FALSE?

True: Green energy uses renewable resources that don't run out, such as wind, sunlight or ocean waves.

The second statement is false.

PAGE 47
ARE YOU A HEAT HOTSHOT?
1B, 2B, 3A

PAGE 55
AIR: TOTALLY TRUE OR FOOLISHLY FALSE?

The first statement is false.

True: Certain trees, such as elms and ashes, can filter out air pollutants, reducing city smog.

PAGE 59
ARE YOU AIR AWARE?
1A, 2B, 3A

FIND OUT MORE

Check out **panda.org** to find out how the World Wide Fund for Nature is tackling climate change to protect our animals.

Ask an adult if you can look up **Greta Thunberg**'s official Facebook or Twitter account to get some green inspiration.

Become a Climate Kid with NASA at **climatekids.nasa.gov**.

Explore your world at **natgeokids.com** and find out how to Reduce, Reuse and Recycle at **recyclenow.com** and **wastebuster.co.uk**.